For Robert Dodd. E.D.

Copyright © 1999 Zero to Ten Limited

Illustrations copyright © 1999 Emma Dodd • Text copyright © 1999 Hannah Reidy

Publisher: Anna McQuinn • Art Director: Tim Foster

Senior Art Editor: Sarah Godwin • Senior Editor: Simona Sideri

First published in Great Britain in hard cover in 1999 by Zero to Ten Limited.

This edition published in 2000 by Zero to Ten Limited

327 High Street, Slough, Berkshire SL1 1TX

ISBN 1-84089-185-8

Printed in Hong Kong.

What noises can you hear?

Written by Hannah Reidy
Illustrated by Emma Dodd

Before her eyes are
even open, Evie can hear

morning noises.

Between bites of her breakfast,
Kesia can just about hear

kitchen noises.

Holding Dad's hand
all the way, Stuart can hear

street noises.

Waiting quietly in the queue,

Lying in the green,
green grass,
Rosie can hear

garden noises.

As silly sister splashes Dad, Beth can hear **bath-time noises.**

Squelch!

Drip!

Tired and tucked up tight,
Nina can hear

night-time noises.

What noises

can **YOU** hear?